My life, you see

SELECTED POEMS

MARTINA THOMSON

Edited by Jane Duran & Sue MacIntyre

HEARING EYE

Published by Hearing Eye 2022
Hearing Eye, Box 1, 99 Torriano Avenue, London NW5 2RX, UK
email: hearing_eye@torriano.org
www.hearingeye.org

ISBN: 978-1-905082-79-7

ACKNOWLEDGMENTS

Eleven of these poems appeared in
Ferryboats (Hearing Eye, 2008).

'Jim Galt' was published in
Long Poem Magazine (LPM), issue 5,
'The River Nairn' in Scintilla, issue 14,
and 'Marion' in Rialto, issue 66.

Cover: ceramic bowl by Martina Thomson
(Photograph: Dave Chapman)

Page vii: two flasks by Martina Thomson
(Photograph: Erica Smith)

Book design: Wordsmith Design
Printed by: YouLovePrint, Uckfield, East Sussex

Distribution:
Central Books, 50 Freshwater Road, Chadwell Heath RM8 1RX

INTRODUCTION

Martina Schulhof was born in Berlin in 1925 to Austrian parents. Just before the Second World War the family left Berlin and came to England. During the war Martina was in boarding school but spent her holidays on a farm in the Cotswolds. The farm left a deep impression on her and inspired her long poem 'Jim Galt':

One day, working in a BBC recording studio in Birmingham, I overheard two men who had come in from a village nearby talking about Jim Galt: '… now works on the roads, uses the Falcon', and was surprised by the emotional effect this had on me. Jim Galt had been the farmer on the farm where my mother had taken rooms when she was bombed out in London. I was evacuated at school but was allowed home for the holidays and this was my first full experience of the country. I learned to milk, took part in the farm work and was utterly taken by it all, by the farmer too.

When with this release of feelings I let my memory speak, sections of the poem came to me one by one – cowshed, dairy, and what was it about the landscape that held me so strongly?

I seemed as though I was making something solid out of shifting images.*

Martina trained at RADA, acted using the stage name Martina Mayne, and in 1952 met the celebrated writer, BBC producer and folklorist David Thomson, whom she married in 1964. With their three sons, they made their home in Camden Town and rented an old schoolhouse in Norfolk. They also spent time in Scotland, Ireland and Greece.

In the '70s Martina trained as an art therapist, later writing *On Art and Therapy*, published by Virago in 1989. She became a gifted potter, experimenting with different glazes and forms. After her husband's death in 1988 she devotedly managed his literary estate.

Although Martina had always kept diaries, she came to writing poetry late in life. She threw herself into this new vocation. She joined Jane Duran's workshop, initially based at the Poetry Society, which she attended religiously until shortly before she died in 2013. She was also a participant in Mimi Khalvati's poetry workshops and seminars. Having entered the world of poetry, Martina became utterly dedicated to it and indeed was distressed when she felt unable to write: *When I found myself unable to write a poem I decided to look over my old diaries for inspiration and was surprised how what I had noted down, from entry to entry, began to take on a somewhat surreal quality.***

In 2008 Hearing Eye published her pamphlet *Ferryboats*, and in 2012 *Panther and Gazelle*, her lucid translations of the German poet Paula Ludwig.

Martina became our close friend and part of the 'family' of Jane's workshop. Her diffidence and warmth, humour and generosity, wide reading and curiosity were unique. She hosted a number of workshops in her Camden Town home, among her beautiful ceramics. After classes at the Poetry Society in Betterton Street, she enjoyed wandering round the city streets at night, and on one occasion, already in her eighties, she joined in the celebrations in Trafalgar Square when Algeria had qualified for the World Cup.

Martina developed bone cancer, which she wrote about courageously and even humorously. She died of pneumonia in 2013 at the age of 88, leaving behind an extensive collection of poems, mostly unpublished.

We greatly admired her work and felt that it should be read more widely. With a view to publication we decided to share the many poems out among members of Jane's workshop who helped with the selection.

Some poems had a number of versions, and where it was not clear which was the preferred one we had to make editorial choices. Our selection naturally fell into an order that reflected the stages of Martina's life. These deeply felt, beautiful poems draw vividly and honestly on her rich life and her attachments to people and places.

Jane Duran and Sue MacIntyre

* from the introduction to 'Jim Galt' in LPM, Issue 5
** from the introduction to 'Visit to Mr James' in LPM, Issue 9

§

Our thanks to Jane's workshop group for their advice and enthusiastic support for this book; to Lynne Hjelmgaard who was of invaluable assistance in organising the text; to Martin Parker for his help in the early stages of the book; to Erica Smith for her excellent book design; and to Susan Johns and Emily Johns of Hearing Eye.

JD and SM

Contents

"Let words so settle down."

Lilac

The lilac I planted bloomed this year,
clusters of white, a scent I remember.

There were so many at the back of the house
in the alcove where I buried my dolls,

the two together in a shoebox. Bakelite dolls,
I could not love them but gave them ceremony.

Are they still there? I'll return to the echoey station
where the engine shuddered, where I moved among grown-ups,

to the streets near the house, cobblestone streets,
their names go Lohengrin, Parsifal, Tristan.

They gave us a yellow star. Unlatch the garden gate,
up three steps, then in, among the lilacs, my secret act.

Clown Drawing

Suddenly I have it in my hand,
postcard size, the glass

now cracked, my father
had it framed, but why?

Pencil lines, a smile, a pointed hat
checkered red and blue

and underneath, oh look,
in large, undaunted letters –

the spiky script I'd learned –
my name, that early name,

which has so well been lost.
I blow the dust off and look close:

it's the classroom that I see
and striving on the blackboard

the angled Gothic writing long obsolete
which still stirs in my wrist.

I'm alone here with my find –
is no one in the house?

Sundays

On Sunday mornings the bathroom was the place to be,
here, to see my mother and my aunt
dance round each other in the steam
as they stepped into the bath to take their shower,
their nakedness up close. My mother's breasts
were apples, she was fair, the water silvered her,
my aunt was olive skinned, her breasts were long
and hung like pears as from a wind-blown branch.

Her arm outstretched had darkness at its root,
between her legs the dark shape that I looked for
and only here on Sundays dark hair fell about her –
I'd spin out time and brush my teeth forever.
Their words came out too loud or muffled by the drains;
then the towelling chapter, the good smell from the powder
which puffed them from the room in shapeless gowns.

Soon after them my father took his bath.
I've seen him lie there long, his head made pink,
offered on a rubber pillow, and half-way down his length
the flannel he kept floating in just that position
and never shifted even though I asked.
But he was easy in the bathroom, sang
his Russian song and teased me and I liked it.

When guests arrived for coffee, cake, the endless talk
and ping-pong in the garden, my family made me shy –
to have them glisten so, the way they leant back
in their chairs, pursed their lips or twisted, stretched
to take a light, the way they threw their laughter out
like questions – were they given to water still?
The morning steam gleamed and hung.

Night-watch

My grandmother unwrapped her legs as she sat,
a snow mountain, on my mother's bed.

I watched her in pretended sleep
from the mattress I camped on for her visit.

Over and under she unwound the bandage
from above her knee down to her ankle,

round and about, a fairy-tale task,
the roll growing clumsy in her hands.

They were boneless legs all softness and
goodness, seal-pups pitted like porridge

which she folded away into the bolsters.
The bedsprings sang as they received her.

When the light was out, I heard her prayer.

Zucker und Zimt

for my grandmother

She held it in her hands as a potter holds clay,
the warm yeast dough for Apfelstrudel,
dumped it on the damask she'd spread on the table,
began to knead in a rock-a-bye motion.
Small nibbles were allowed from the raisins in the bowl,
the pared, sliced apples, the *Zucker und Zimt*.

And now with the rolling-pin the work of a master:
she began from the middle, pushed out her fabric
always from the middle, like a tide it reached further,
a domain expanding with soft, scalloped edges
growing pearly, precious, a baby skin, see-through
it annexed and possessed the entire stretch –
hands to her back in relief when she'd done,
her smile and her nod for me to begin.

At once all fingers into the apples,
fistfuls to be dropped on to the dough-cloth
evenly, evenly, and again and again, then I rained
down the raisins, seed-scattered the bread-crumbs
and from the height of my silver spoon cruising
bestowed the valediction, the *Zucker und Zimt*.

A *pas de deux* followed, one each side of the table
we lifted the damask, unsaddled the dough-cloth,
in measured pavane we nudged the thing forward
so it rolled and enfolded its bulky harvest.
Step by step the roll expanded till its stuffed belly
slumped. My grandmother made it a crescent moon.

5

Frau Trümpler

The sewing machine was set up by the window in the
Kinderzimmer. When we heard it was Frau Trümpler's
day, we thumped up the stairs, then paused at the door,
entered shyly because we knew we'd look – first thing – to
see whether her two 'angels' sat in place on the
windowsill. And there they were, two dumpy white paper
bags, each with two ears, two wings twisted up. She was
round and dumpy herself and smiled and never forgot. She
lived above the sweet-shop. The wicker basket was stacked
with her things: sheets and towels to patch, my father's
collars to turn, Tom's torn pockets, the hems of my frocks.
I liked to settle by her on the floor and journey along, her
knee making the engine buzz – start-stop, run-stop – and
when a sheet came down and folded me in, I travelled in
her boat, picked out a raspberry sweet. Two passengers
stood beside me, Frau Trümpler's feet in plum lisle
stockings and blunt shoes – strangers.

Tristanstrasse

The milk-cart rattles over cobblestones,
the high, clear sound of Hübner's bell,
froth to the brim in the jug they hold,
rides can be cadged, the pony stroked.

Then milk-vans come on rubber tyres,
'hurry up, quick,' a hooter calling,
blunt bottles handed over coldly –
still it is summer and she loves her frocks.

But listen, black boots now click in the street,
a staccato flagsong disrupts the day.
The dog is poisoned, lies yelping and dies
while their father keeps vigil stretched on the sofa.

From her desk at school she sees a man fall
across the window: a pause in the classroom.
'A shop's been burgled, the church is on fire!'
'Ah, you don't know', says the piano teacher.

Suddenly packers are in their house:
she runs to the garden to bury her dolls.
Thomas goes away to an English school,
when winter comes she too is sent.

Their room in London is in that street
where the buildings all look exactly the same.
Her tongue dances a new language in her mouth
and she makes a secret of her childhood words.

Father

Behind him the bushes
Close their branches
The grass rises up
Solitude takes him.
                    Goethe

A grazing of your hand you told us
hurts more than a bullet passing through the body.
You lay and waited on the battlefield
a cornfield and the sky was blue –
on that you would insist.
Cornfield and sky were your concern,
that's where you were bedded.
You watched no pageant of your life –
it was the midday sky.
An antiseptic stabbing of the wound
awoke you; and at dawn the wagons left,
you saw them every morning
stacked with corpses,
canvas sheeting thrown across
but at the back
the rigid legs stuck out.
How did they take you to Tashkent?
When did your prisoner's life
there in the salt-works
start to please you and seem rich –
a touchstone in your memory
voiced in your Russian song?
Forgive me for the questions that I never asked.

§

I know so little about you,
see you mostly lying on the sofa
arms folded up around your head,
blue smoke rings opening, rising.
'More' we said, and you made more.
Then the long night our dog lay stretched out
on the floor beside you, whimpering, yelping.
Did his poisoning make you face the emigration?

Dr Schwoner and Dr Weinberg, your old friends,
twin guests at Sunday lunch, no longer came.
Dr Schwoner with the injured hand
dead like a beetle on its back
was found dead in his room.
Dr Weinberg went to Israel
made a garden in the desert and sent a box
of oranges which when we opened it
glowed like a sunrise in the house.
The neighbour said he must not greet you any more.
You told me that.

In your book-filled room above your desk
a death-mask on the wall, landscape
of rounded forehead and closed lids
secret streamlet of the lips. Its whiteness
and its silence made me see it as your head.
I wish you knew though that I still breathe in
the smell I love of smoke and sweat
of thumb and finger as you strewed the sleepy-sand
first searched for in your pocket
into the corners of my eyes. And my belief:
yes, I would sleep.

Wannsee 1938

The staircase at the end of the corridor,
barren like everything else in the school –

nothing absorbent about it or mellow,
nothing muddled like home –

and all the time breathing the green shiny paint,
the child left behind with a leg that hurts –

the hundred steps down from where she squats –
one at a time on her bottom

nearer and nearer to the sound of hammering,
little spurts of metallic sound.

The hall is empty, the children have gone,
will the men in uniform let her pass?

They call her over, show her the nails,
the black ones, the white ones, the red,

and say she's to hammer a nail in the emblem –
flag that stands for her father's death –

to give them her coin for their crime.
Proud to be handed a sparkling hammer,

she picks a red nail, pins it to the pattern,
hammers straight – while her heart says 'no' –

helps to hoist the iron banner,
pierces her father with every stroke.

Children's Home

It was almost night-time when the party started, the sky grown dark; out in the garden paper lanterns hung from branches, lanterns made like concertinas folded up around a candle, some had faces, some were moons. A golden drink was ladled from a goldfish bowl and this place that was so far from home and so unhappy was made new. The ladies that so troubled us in uniform, in their party frocks had turned invisible. We too were now unseen, had ceased to matter, were left free to wander. Visitors had arrived and lay outside in deck chairs. Officers stepped over from the camp; men's voices gave the undertone. The air was loose and easy, yet whatever was hatched out was of importance and from below the grassy bank came little runs of laughter and something that was murmured.

Toffee

For a penny at Woolworths
you got ten toffees
and I practised how to say
'Have a sweet', like the others.
And it worked: 'Oh have a sweet'.

I learned the speech from Gettysburg:
'Four score and twenty years ago'
and could recite it, but
we said it in a chorus with Mr Harwood
out in front conducting us.

Mr Harwood always held his head
to one side and I loved it
when he said 'Now children'
and when he said 'cathedral'.
It was the r's that were so funny,

my tongue did acrobatics
so to roll them. I think his head
sat crooked on too short a neck.
He was very English, I think a gentleman.

Jim Galt

That was the summer of 'The Idiot',
my encampment in the hayloft.
My brother found me, with a treasure
in his hand, a crinkled photograph

he'd pulled out of the sofa
and it was of our Jim Galt
with harrow and two horses
halfway up the now untended field

and he was naked
and it showed his buttocks.

§

Shuffle and touch, enclosed in the half-dark:
flicker of oil lamp, wind at the thatch,

as each cow homes to her place at the trough,
a reaching and nudging to fasten the chain,

my head to the nook between ribcage and thigh,
a pressure against me of heartbeat and breath,

hands warm on teats, each known for its feel,
release of milk, thrum in the bucket.

A mothering smell at dawn and at dusk.

§

Who would paint the dairy:
the cool air as we entered,
ivory white of plastered walls,
silver sparkle of the churns,
the spareness and the order,
antithesis of cowshed?

Who'd paint the milk we brought in
swaying in the bucket,
froth that covered it, the blue
it gathered as it spread,
ran thinly down the cooler:
the blue veins of baby skin,

and the solemnity of place,
the laboratory where what we'd taken
from the cow, the cow's warm gift,
was neutralised and measured –
who'd paint the dairy empty?

§

Waltzing Matilda, waltzing Matilda,
You'll come a-waltzing, Matilda, with me –

His voice a challenge to the rough descent,
he stood heroic, the reins in his hand,
the milk-float surfing under his feet
down across the sparkling field,
Bessy's canter the joy of the morning.

He left the milk churns at the corner stand,
unyoked the pony in the butcher's yard,
took a short-cut through the slaughterhouse,
had me trail him past the heavy hangings –
I left him at the Public Bar.

At the turn of the day, Bessy brought home
the empty churns and a voided man;
the hush of evening, of hillside and night-sky
folded us in at milking time.

§

After work the four slow men
pushed their black bikes up the hill,
their steps considered, their very movements
a philosophy. In the winter
in the early dark, light from their headlamps
flitted here and there like creatures
of the road. Words came out in phrases
known between them, in several voices,
the refrains almost awaited.
This was said and that, marked the stages
of the road as did the church,
the graveyard, the cemetery further up
and then Jim Galt's, his patch
of mangel-wurzels, *not much to the kale*,
the oak tree where the postman left the letters –
a place for bats, shadow dancers,
quick against the measure of the men.

Past the bend, on both sides of the road,
it was the Purdy Acres, a climb they mostly
took in silence, a ritual stepping, thoughts
their own, cold air against the skin,
sometimes the stars, the moon and rain –
hands firm on handlebars, their faces down.
A change came with the turning to the village.
There were some comforts here and night
was not so close.

§

The stillness of the place was in colours,
subdued, toned down, as if the Lady Murasaki

had thrown her veil across to make them reticent
since in her land the sumptuous, riotous hues

were dulled to quieten intoxication, rein in
the outward pull, render absence, loneliness.

Evening yellow rose, yellow rose fragrance,
fragrant pink-plum layer, flowery pink-plum –

a hundred and seventy names for colours
and the killing of them to make black.

The beauty of the farmland was
at one remove, was hesitant.

§

I want the fields that rise up
to the farm all to be vertical,
stacked one upon the other;
they're a woven fabric, rectangles
and squares of greens, greys, browns –
all are immediate and speak together;
don't allow them to explain themselves,
stretch back into the distance,
but have them rise and rise,
almost fill the canvas to the top
where a narrow field of sky
is taking blue thread for a border.

No, let that be, there is no border,
the reach goes on, the field
we call Moon-Acres still expands.

The whole thing is a cloth
I want to lay against my face:
the comfort it would give…
The farmhouse, yellow-grey,
with its surrounding wall sits high up
on the left exactly where I've known it
over years and here the motley cows
drawn in around the elm, so innocent.

November Meeting with my Father

We breathed in steam, the smell of fish frying,
bubbling oil to the left as I faced you,

the window out to the dark fogged-up.
The steam enclosed us. *Tchish* in the tea-urn.

You'd said 'meet you there', and I came off the bus,
I'd something to tell you, my life, you see. My life

just beginning. And I'd failed and must tell you.
You worked in this town, I in another, not far.

We both were teaching, my class in chaos –
I gave you the letter which gave me notice,

my eyes on your thumbnail while you were reading,
the one that sat crooked – your war-wounded hand.

And my father looked up and he smiled.

The Bookbinder

The name Van Gogh in large green capitals
on fawn, cut from the book my mother has re-bound,
is pasted on the cover. She took grey linen
for the binding and I see her struggle to make good –
the way the endpapers are strained to line
the inside of the boards. I like this imperfection,
hear her breathing as she glues and sews together
pages that had fallen apart – shoulders bent,
the right always ahead, as in her crab-like walk
when suddenly she flipped down to pick a bit of green
or fallen blossom from the pavement, held
between her fingers like an offering till she found
a hedge, a patch of earth or grass to vouchsafe
a softer death – so obstinate in her care.

My Father's Words

He left his desk; his writing
   had disappeared behind the paper,
     had reached the not-said.

With the door locked behind him
   he walked across a winter field,
     looked down at the sea from a rock.

'Never to come to a clear position
   and yet to bear it – and may I come
     to love this unsatisfied yearning?'

Was this what he asked in his book,
   the book he'd carried across the Alps,
     the one he was always writing?

He hurried ahead, found the gap to a steep
   descent where, with the wind at him
   and stung by driving sand,
     he struggled down exalted.

In June

after Gerhard Richter

From the land of orange-red
tumbling, green shoots spring.

A folding of green shoots
layer on layer – is there a core?

I see it, know it, perched up in the
golden section, a little cabin –

companion to my days
in a field of flux.

The Potter

I work with clay
coil on coil
joining, judging.

My ear to the inner wall
as it makes a hollow
curves and stretches.

Always the touch
clay to fingers
a current of pleasure.

Chance marks on the outside
speak of secrets
guide my hand.

Decorations are incantations
to call forth magic
invite a blessing.

I find, lose, find
then something that I recognise
the moment I see it.

And now the alchemical fire.

Glaze Test

The contours of three brushstrokes
on my test piece are edged

in orange by iron oxide
which glaze and flame

have wakened in the clay,
fine, wavering lines

as if traced in pencil
by Morandi. And so

the line a hill draws
in the sky has thrilled me,

ever-shifting versions
as I walk towards it –

so many goes at touch
and demarcation.

That Year

1955 was the year of Paris –
spring, summer and into autumn –
Paris Soir! Paris Soir! was my canto,
high on the smell of Gauloises and garlic,
with pastis, Pernod, transubstantiation,
ice-cold potion that flamed in the chest.
Long skirts were out, the New Look old,
the shift I lived in I bought on Boule' Miche,
clip-clop all day in strap-mad sandals.
I picked up some funds dubbing in films,
I picked up lice in my lousy hotel.
Existential on Sartre, raw on Camus,
days at the Chaumière (a franc in the turnstile),
tiers and tiers of students drawing,
the air a-sizzle with concentration,
you had to be quick to catch the short poses,
shed pages and pages of flimsy newsprint,
then out on the Boulevard, the café in favour,
we slung back the menu in student canteens.
That summer surely was sunny and hot,
we bared our feet to stretch on the grass
though that was the one thing *défendu*.
Living and breathing was exultation,
all was seductive, sex in a muddle,
so dizzy I liked what I saw in the mirror,
how easy it was to fall in love…

Rue du Cotentin

'I destroyed it,' I said out loud
at the thought of our life in that attic –
the back room all bed, pure celebration,
the wide view over shuntings, the horses.
At first, far away, like a bubbling of water,
then louder and hammering, calling out
echoes – they came, so many, alongside
the hoarding, down to the goods yard
abreast on the road. How I watched
their sleek backs from our high window,
held there till the last straggler had passed.

Years later, by the time I had spoilt so much,
smitten as I was with another man,
and had left that beautiful funny flat,
I knew the horses were for the slaughter.
You saw that I loved them and held it from me.

Words on the Move

She walks with the book
held open before her
and in it reads
story after story.

The wood she comes to,
fence and gate,
the sodden place,
the bird in the branches,

these are her stories.
She closes the book –
hears footsteps inside her.

A Story

He brought her back to make her his wife.
She did not consent but liked the adventure.

He folded her to him, held her close.
She felt she could swim in his summer smell.

He held out a towel for her after her bath.
She preferred to dive to the warmth of his body.

His eyes followed a baitish girl.
Hers fell to the ground with him up to his tricks.

He corrected her English, taught her the conditional.
'But I'd know how to use it, should I want to use it.'

His handwriting was clear, performed elegant loops.
Hers full of gaps barely touched the page.

His pages made books, his books filled shelves.
She moulded clay, played with the river.

He saw her, a seal, swim out to the sea.
She saw him, a hare, leap up to the moon.

Blue Door

I'm looking for the blue door you once gave me,
tongue and groove, two stone steps up,
a narrow door that leads into a garden.

This is the path that runs along the plane trees –
and here the wall which bounds this out-stretch of the park.

You'd seen me stand so long and longingly
in front of that small watercolour drawing,
a framed page, lifted from her sketchbook –

Mary Potter's 'Blue Door in a Wall'.
And so you brought me here,
made this garden door your gift.

Under hazel branches a mattress on the ground,
a bit of shelter pitched against the cold.

Trinity Island

A wooded island, silent and dark –
there's sadness for me in this
stillness that won't let me go.

I'm like the woman further up by Lough Key
always in front of the fire, watching
the small quiet flames of the turf.

This must be the path we took, in
beyond the ash trees. I want to walk
the same way – a mild celebration.

There are buds here on the branches
yet it's so cold. What is this vim
that can push out buds in this greyness?

When a storm broke on the lake, we rowed
for all we could with only one aim –
to bring the children safe to the shore.

The Stone in his Pocket

He let his thumb follow the curve of it,
move down to where it flattened
to what he called the lobe, which wet

down by the sea had glistened pink
and which he often licked
to give it back its colour.

The hollow of the stone, the little dent,
he saved for last, it gave him pleasure.
For this was Jenny's ear,

the Sunday Jenny who he saw in church,
whose name he knew but who
he'd never spoken to.

Vis-à-vis

There's air in a Bonnard, but here
you've trapped me in a Hopper painting,
blocked me with angled perspectives,
blanked the outlook, silenced our talk.

Where's play, where ornament,
the lightness I love, the flighty business
of ease, charm and seduction?
Where dance? What can quicken

in a realm forever arrested?
No breathing in this fixture.
I'm stifled by unsaid words,
my voice a sickness I carry

with the frugal teapot that serves us
and you across the table, thin.

Journey

Ultramarine or midnight blue and black
the colours he'd long worked for – now
his prize – this darkest midnight blue.

And he embarks. The boat will travel westward
leaving mainlands far behind –
then north-northwest into a lighter sea. Clarity

will be the substance of the air he breathes.
He knows the journey well, has dreamt it often
can see the route the boat makes on the map

and now waits for the first view of the island.
There he'll walk on close-cropped grassy slopes
beside stone walls, where sheep look up, small birds

white-breasted, rise from the heather. There he will rest.
The boat drops anchor in the island harbour
commotion, voices, ropes, the gangplanks down

small boats converge, to fetch, to carry
but he stands lamed by indecision – remains on board.
And journeys on into a haze that blinds him.

He fingers in his pocket a midnight blue.

Leave-taking

Was it absence you sought
  when you turned from the road
to stand on the banks
  of the Findhorn, with the house
of Polloghaig on the far side,
  The House of Three Candles
hidden in fir trees or gone,
  where the chain-ferry beside you
stood rusted and locked
  and no horse would come
to fetch you across?

Days, Years

I've lost my days,
maybe I've squandered them.
Monday, Tuesday, Wednesday –
they escaped. Sunday
I held fast, gave it
the grassy slope wrapped
in early mist, gave it
the beech leaves tinged
with orange, each one single,
drawn into itself,
offered the hush, the holiness
of entering the wood
where birch trees glowed
not white but blue,
blue-grey.
    I've lost my years
but not the year I lost you
that stands like the onset
of a winter, drawn into itself.

The River Nairn

in memory of David Thomson

With the wretched thing under my arm
I left the house early, walked
the high path along the Nairn,

then scrambled down to a sandbank
where the water played
over stones, a game of shadow and light,

stepping stones that brought me a good way in
so that I stood midstream for the business
of letting your ashes go.

God – I wanted to swallow a mouthful,
strewed a handful in my hair, gravelly stuff,
not the mild ash that might absolve a sinner.

The rest was carried away in the rush
of small galloping waves
that the wind had whipped up.

Away, past green banks tucked in among alders
where you'd stood beside Michie, the wild man
– long days of fishing, of boyhood –

beyond the graveyard up on its ridge,
past the town, the campsite, the harbour,
away out to sea, sea of the selchie

that had so often enticed you away.

The Missing Poet

A streak of pump-water –
so thin, would he last the winter?
You feared he might break in half.
But he held to, was pliant,
most so when a girl's face pleased him –
the widest smile, the sparkle
of his eyes made precious, many times
refracted by glasses within glasses,
goggle-specs. Blind in the dark
he groped, his arm outstretched,
toes testing the ground.

He walked the streets of Camden,
an ally of vagrants and winos,
entered pubs for pints of draught bitter,
his pockets bulged with notebooks.
You'd think him absentminded
when you saw him pick up a matchbox,
turn it between thumb and finger,
gaze at it long from all angles –
what was he dreaming of?
The streets lack grace without him,
this wanderer, this poet.

In Camden Town

The shoemaker's widow and the widow
of the milkman on their daily round,

the frail one always a little ahead –
I watch them as I sit at your desk.

It's the wind rattles the door.
You lurk in places where I don't

expect you, in the names of streets,
pubs and hospitals – it tears my body

and later I know we've been there.
This morning in the park I passed

through a strait of your presence,
the regimented tulip display

that was our joke – did you take me
for the blue filly in your book,

the way you ran your hand down my face?
I walked by the ragged border where

the hellebore leaves are in shreds,
a swarm of brown teasels

against the sky; I saw the wolves
trot back and forth in their enclosure.

Winter

He'd come back,
had come down the farm track
between its two stone walls,
walked into the house,
made the room glow –
and I knew I was forgiven.
It made all the difference.
And then he left again,
took the lower track,
walked out of my sight.
With the saddest heart
I knew not to follow him.

Holkham Bay

Yesterday at Holkham I watched the tide come in:
rivulets of brown, bubbly water spilling over ridges

and running along, two or three at a time
that then linked with others reaching across.

The next moment my patch of beach was under water
and there seemed to be an in-breath, a pause.

But at once a new wave brought new impulse
and the tide fingers explored new runs:

a fast, an effortless game, releasing to watch.
And there, oh yes, I felt close to you –

the unstoppable tide and that wide, boundless beach
on which we'd once walked together.

David

Your chair I can touch now, it doesn't attack me,
your coat still hangs there but has no power.
All around here what there was is expended.
You don't disturb me. Perhaps I'm forgetting you.

But there's no safety on the roads beyond Galway
where snipers linger at crossroads – signposts
with names barely familiar target my chest.
Spiddal, Oughterard, Carraroe and Carna.

Sleepwalker, I'm drawn to the pub by the pier,
the one with the fish-shed askew beside it,
and on entering know we sat here –
I take the black drink of your absence.

Tiree

Step out here where air and light
entice you to an exploration –

ground is springy under your feet,
clumps of grass – pungent green,

patches too of mud and water;
stones, a hillside built of boulders –

a herd of rounded bodies,
a huddle of light grey pelts

lie resting one against the other
stretched towards the coast; night

and day, the weight, the everlastingness.
At times black sheep appear

stark on the ridge behind you,
survey the stretch of land

and bleat. A grassy scalloped
valley draws down to the cove –

the distant in-and-out breath of the sea.

Islanders

Where now the beach is murkiest –
shallow, fouled with plastic rubbish
and the carcass of a sheep –
was once the landing stage.
From here a track, partly paved, leads up
past the farmyard to the house,
the big house of the island.

How will I remember it?
The fences mostly down,
there are no horses in the home-field,
the stabling has no cows, the chicken coops
are empty, and the dramatic turkey
whom I always circumvented
is nowhere. The house itself is let
with shooting rights. Its owner
has retreated to the mainland.

Little remains: four cottages, a barn,
a church, at times a ferry.
Last year there were eight islanders,
this year there are seven. And I mourn
the tall free-striding one who loved boats
and built one – his bolt-hole, and sanctum.

Clearances

The path runs high above the sea
across a stretch of moorland.
There are no sheep now on the island –

no profit in them to the laird –
and I do miss them, and their close-cropped grass,
both my special loves.

I miss the startled scramblings,
two or three together, the bell-like sound
light feet call from stone,

the constant pulling at the grass
and the sudden looking up –
the surprise of night skies in those eyes.

Bracken, fiery brown now at the end of summer
has taken all the slopes; and down
towards the water's edge are other absences

marked by ruins of the tumbled houses –
the mill, the school, the church.

Homefield

It is a field that stretches
away to the east. It's bound
by a ditch of water.

The clouds in the water
tremble with the wind,
tentative.

Forget-me-nots are crossing
the ditch, spurs of buddleia
cling to the edge. A blue glow

flees across the grass and trails
on the far-off fence, it does this
again and again. I'm waiting

for Celia but have in my mind
her small wickerwork coffin,
frail and light, as she was.

Marion

You'd moved your bed down and now slept among
the spades and buckets, beanpoles, trowels, baskets –
there the new commode and, yes, the glass door to the garden.

You sat bolt upright on the crumpled sheets
and when I greeted you I found your cheek
was wet with tears: 'Forgive me if I don't get up,'

your eyes without your specs so intimate, so bare.
A letter had arrived. 'The second drawer
up in the tallboy, you'll see it, bring it down' –

a letter spun of accusations. 'So, what d'you make of it?'
'I want to put my arms round you, that's all.'
'Well then –' and now your tears were hot.

Your heartbeat stayed with me when you drew back;
there was a stillness in the room and dusk,
the gardening tools lost contour, substance –

shadows of a chorus closed around us
and you now with the wicked lightening of your smile,
the tilted head: 'I think that's drowned that letter.'

Ready for the whisky, we raised the tumblers eye to eye.
You told me you'd found words, end words, for your chapter
which made the book complete. We toasted it

on this last night. Oh Marion, you wanted me to stay
but then said: 'No, come see me when it's day.'

Breakfast with Anna

Her hands passed out the white folded cloth,
tanned old hands, ruckled silk,
    why so vivid her broad gold ring?

A concrete path outside her cabin,
small octagonal iron table,
    hands again, two plates, two cups.

Officiating hands through the open window,
a lidded dish for her pat of butter,
    stronger and stronger the smell of coffee.

You reach me my childhood, you reach me the war,
your life now stilled in this mountain village,
    filament of awe, live wire of love.

Poppy-seed rolls the baker had left,
honey we'd fetched from the hive up the valley,
    a lifting of the monstrance with the coffee done.

She placed the jug on the windowsill,
worked fingers on white porcelain,
    and then she came round and we began.

Schneeberg

She lived with a sense of Snowmountain.
She would open the curtains to see –
had new snow covered the slopes?
Were they hidden in mist, in rain?
Did the peak rise above clouds,
wear a gold crown in the sun?
Bent now with eyes to the ground
she knew it had witnessed her raptures.

Village in the midst of maize fields
where cows were kept locked in dark sheds,
a village surveyed by Snowmountain,
its own elect guardian, that gave
weight to the villagers' greetings:
'God bless, how he stands clear.'

New Snow on the Mountain

Anna was lying on the couch
by the window, the remains of a dream.
In words I bent down to she told me
she'd brought the oleander in,
where I would find the folder
with the letters and how I must carry her
to some altar place when she was dead.
Her death was the slightest shift.

I lifted her body, which was light,
resting on my arms like a casket
structured of moth-wings –
white, grey and violet.

Wells Tavern

They met where they'd met some years ago.
    He was expecting her and when she entered

came to meet her. She knew at once the place
    had changed, the quiet pub now loud with laughter,

but as for him, she was not sure, she felt detached
    and watched him. After a while she recognised

the phrases, the old emphases – saw the cards laid out
    and didn't want to play. They left together,

walked out into the cold, silence rising from the trees.
    He wrote to say their meeting had been simple,

irresistible like the seasons – spring and summer,
    autumn, change and dissolution.

A Western Woman's First Things

She fumbles for her watch under her pillow
squints and sees it's half past six
tosses and turns, rolls over twice
throws off the blankets, puts her feet on the floor
nice feel of carpet, cold feel of lino
arrived in the bathroom applies seat to seat
handles the roll, all it implies
depresses the lever, hears the sound of the flush
steps in the bath, turns the tap of the hot
gives a half-turn to the cold, lets her fingers judge
squeezes the bottle of precious shower gel
lets her palm receive the creamy oozings
lets her nose breathe in the seductive smell
pats her body with the stuff in requisite places
lets the water run down, all down the old body
she's had for long, she's had it for long
rubs with her hand to make it clean
rinses it now so it's fresh and done
steps out on the bath-mat, reaches up for the towel
rub-a-dub-dub, more here, more there
back on the carpet, she opens the drawer
takes out clean pants, swaddles her bottom
strains to fasten the hooks of her brassiere
pulls up her tights, steps into her jeans
arms and shoulders twist into her vest

covers with zip top, zips up the zip
boots, one each, for each of her feet
takes hairbrush and comb to tackle her hair
takes mirror to see, puts it down straight away
searches for the house keys, finds her specs
with them in her hand she's ready to go
free hand on the banisters, a look through the window
she steps down first five steps, then nine and nine
arrived in the hallway she walks to the front door
inserts the key, turns it round in the lock
unhooks the chain with which he once blessed her
makes for the kitchen over creaky floorboards
fills the kettle from the cold tap, depresses the switch
opens the cupboard, takes out small saucepan
again some water from the same tap, today is Tuesday
her one-a-week egg, she's decided on boiled
puts the brownest in the saucepan, the saucepan on the gas ring
small struggle with cooker to light up the gas
ditto struggle with the grill, overcomes its tantrum
lifts lid off the bread bin, takes out the loaf
places on bread board, cuts with bread knife
takes up slices, positions on grill tray
takes a deep breath. Is she thankful to God?

Kosta's Garden

We are multiple, incoherent
and contradictory.
                    Fernando Pessoa

A scattered herd of bins and buckets, buckets,
  bakers' trays – all afternoon he scrubbed
    each one with soapsuds, going at it like a task
of expiation; now they're stacked, the brown,
  the green, with ladders posted up like turrets,
    old For Sale signs scuttled on the ground.
The butler's sink, I watched him bring that in,
  manoeuvre it around, stand long in admiration –
    perhaps it was a pond before his eyes
with goldfish rising in the shade of irises.
  Dapper in white shirt and jerkin, his clothes hang out
    for purity, for air, days and nights on railings,
stiff in snow the same shirts and the same pyjamas.
  These filchings he's amassed, all this untidy stuff,
    it needles me. And yet I'm hooked, as if
this garden were an offprint of my mind.

In Praise of Stillness

I praise the stillness of the room –
how it so quietly contains
the books strewn on the floor,
the papers I cannot order,
the pots pushed into corners.
While I was absent, how it made peace
in my chaos, laid a patina
on clutter – how poignant
the angle of the shoe by the sink,
how its blue is picked up
by the stain on the table
which again ties over to the toppled
footstool – this stillness
that turned mess into still life –
I step into a classic composition.

A First Entry

This is my new book,
a little smaller than I like,
the lines a little darker,
still, a handsome book,
specially bought and since –
5:30 now – I woke,
I must initiate it with an entry:
Bonjour, bonjour,
mes delices, mon amour...

I'll note down this and that,
a cow, for instance,
delicate, bedecked
with strings of pearl,
a holy cow, a Tamil bronze –
her head held high is crowned,
her admirable weighty spread
makes good the ground she rests on.
Let words so settle down.

Milk Jug

In a dark shop in Kathmandu
I bought a Tibetan milk jug.

It stands here on my kitchen table,
a hollowed trunk straight up,

no sign of lip or spout,
carved round with plaited bands

and rows of diamond shapes
wherever there was room. And look,

a monkey handle, and looped across
a waxed rope to swing it by.

This white streak here, that eats
into the wood, is where the milk

ran down. Yaks' milk, remember.
Come, put your nose inside

and take deep breaths –
the smoky sour smell…

After-image

The birch has spun a dark pink cocoon
my pen writes green letters on invisible pages
closed eyelids spawn deep-sea protozoa.

A blue disk lies down on a dazzling sun
a cloudless sky plays with torn pink shadows
the sun will set soon.

A half-sun sends rays through silver branches –
a tree transfigured, a brief revelation –
down, only down, a fraction, a sparkling.

An echo of orange as the evening opens.
I return to myself – where have I been –
remember my book.

Rapallo

When one really feels or thinks,
one stammers with simple speech.
I read that last night
sitting at the kitchen table
piled with the library books
I'd brought home, too many,
how can I read them all?
But even as they lie there, some open,
some stacked, two on the chair,
they excite me – a pre-exploration state,
as when you've planned a journey
but haven't yet seen your destination.
Now it's the letters of Ezra Pound.
He writes from Rapallo. I remember Rapallo,
remember the orange grove, and still now
its brilliance, its glow, reaches me here
as something seeps out of these unread books.

Sacrificial Wine Jug

Look here I am, myself, my awkward self,
I strut on beetle legs, just three,
strive forward but stand firm. I boast.

My handle declares 'handle, lift me here,'
it does not doubt itself. My spout
is overlarge, a tongue stretched out.

But look, the loving touch, the decoration
that I bear – I cannot read it – he incised
the questing lines that link but do not close.

My stuff is brass. Fill me with wine and place
me over flame. Await the turning
in my belly – you'll pour the sacrifice.

After Chagall

Was I the only one awake?
All doors were closed,
the houses leaning back
into a village sleep;
the empty street
reached grey into a dream.
The blue, your blue, was skyline,
window, road and roof –
you brushed my cheek with it
and it was night, wide open
to a growing moon.
And so you walked into my view,
stalked on two chicken legs
you, my unlikely bird,
my farmyard fowl –
so insouciant, so true.

From a Painter's Notebook

after Paul Nash

A ship has found a mooring in our room.
Captain and crew were taken by the war.

The black hull waits for me,
a white beside it waits for my companion.

The room has cast its angles in the sea
and has becalmed it.

Outline hems my brush, nothing spills –
the flag hangs limp.

One day I'll catch the sun and moon in my retort,
set them to work above the Wittenham Clumps,

land of long barrows and forgotten gods,
where they will summon a pavane of colours,

my deepest blues and reds, gold, pink –
I feel the stirrings in my wrist.

Still Life with Four Vessels

Zurbarán placed four vessels in a row
on a long table. Darkness caresses them all

and they shine. With this darkness
he traced the rims of the vessels,

shadowed the fluting, stroked the handles –
leaving each object an island of colour.

The four together invoke a harmony
yet each stands alone, in isolation.

There is no story. The objects are constant,
stay ever in the present and endure.

It is the Hour

It is the hour – when lovers' vows
Seem sweet...
                                        Byron

It's light, but early yet,
I lie a while, then know
now is the time.

Why is it so good
to move in a house of sleepers,
to find the bolt, draw it back,

step out and walk away?
I walk across the morning grass.

La Guionie

No drama in this landscape
no call to explore it –
a slope of linden and cherry
caught in a wooded valley
embraced by a ring of blue,
a hammock that holds you
lures you to rest.

'We shall rest', says Sonia to Uncle Vanya
when the troublesome guests have gone.

The wind in the branches
echoes distant seas,
the birds' high singing
insists on this summer day.

Here lies the kitchen garden
worked like a carpet –
leeks, onions, strawberries in flower
much of its growth still secret
under raked earth.

Small Volume of Trakl

The book is there
among the others,
I need it there.

Between its covers lie
unstructured landscapes
of a life...

Brown trees, blue ponds,
deer stepping lightly, lightly,
ivory moon.

A solitary path,
a listening out, glimpses
of the figure of a woman.

Her head bows down,
hands are folded –
death ever close.

A book has crossed
my path and left
a dark blue shadow.

In the Limousin

Under the eaves
a small room
a narrow bed
a skylight of clouds
green fields if I tiptoe
last night the journeying stars.

I store the few things
in empty drawers
hang my shirt on the rail
place my book on the slatted table –
it's simple.

Absolved from a house full of stuff
the stone walls of this cell
soothe – is it a rehearsal?

Drift of clouds and a fly buzzing,
kinship with the island hermit
and the song of his blackbird.

Jonah

In the body of the whale
the ribcage howled.
Blackness rubbed my skin,
my arm reached out for breath –
flung from orientation.
There had been light,
I still remembered it.
God had made light
and had extinguished it.

Blackness

I often ask myself,
when I first settled down
in that long room

with kitchen and table –
when I turned out the light
what was it that glowed?

The blackness was utter,
the densest of aquatints,
but scraped back into it

were silver outlines.
My mind has lost it,
I never see it now,

I wake in a dark room
that will not surprise me.

Walking with my Son Ben
on Hampstead Heath

'To be realistic, let's not attempt the hill,
 let's walk here by the pond' –

the trees now towards autumn, the air
just slightly misty, early dusk and

ducks and coots each single on the water,
their raw and single calls

out into the distance. Distance
and closeness, few words between us.

Thoughts rise, turn playful in this
quiet, a gift to take away.

It was not the hill, but when we'd walked
around the pond, it was a circle made.

Right to the Marrow

I am the object of the notes,
notes carnalised – what I
consist of has been measured;

my blood has been surveyed,
judged and registered, and set
against the marrow of my bones.

The measurers confer:
this marrow gives them trouble,
it is irregular!

They've made it the occasion
of myself, they see it erring
and will set it right.

They cannot set it right,
my marrow is my fate,
it is the soul I walk about with –

and yet they mix their potions,
agglutinate, subtract, minimise and
strengthen, dibble-dabble, flutch,

stand ready to do battle.
I rise, the adversary now,
I bare myself, say 'Here,

here is my body which
contains my bones which in turn
contain the errant marrow. Shoot!'

To my sisters

With this illness and these years
I've stepped into an alien body,
have mislaid the one I knew,
the one I nodded to.
This other hangs on me,
a cutout from the camps –
an honorary acquisition,
I have not earned it yet.
My brotherhood is there,
I've joined you, sisters
and now soon, quite soon…

Lilac Corner

It's white lilac I planted
yet year after year the blossoms first
are dark, dark pink, mauve,
and again I'm disappointed.

Why is it that I want this white,
this looseness and this weightlessness?
It is my childhood garden,
where I was secret and alone.

The corner where forever I am
burying my dolls. You had to make
a choice. They were the ones
to leave behind.

I don't think I was sad.
The looseness and full whiteness
of the blossoms seemed to me
a paradise.

Also by Martina Thomson:

On Art and Therapy: An Exploration. Virago 1989
Republished with a new postscript by the author
Free Association Books 1997

Ferryboats. Torriano Meeting House Poetry Pamphlet N° 54
Hearing Eye 2008

Panther and Gazelle. Poems by Paula Ludwig.
Translated and introduced by Martina Thomson
Hearing Eye 2012

David Thomson's books include:

The People of the Sea. 1954

The Leaping Hare (with George Ewart Evans). 1972

Woodbrook. 1974

In Camden Town. 1983

Nairn in Darkness and Light. 1987

Danny Fox. 1966
and other stories for children

About the Editors

Jane Duran is a poet and translator. Enitharmon has
published five collections of her poetry. Her latest collection,
the clarity of distant things was published by Carcanet in 2021.

Sue MacIntyre's first collection of poetry, *The Wind Today,*
was published by Hearing Eye. Following two pamphlets, her
second full collection, *The woman who couldn't finish things,*
was published by Stonewood Press in 2021.